THE

CHILDREN'S

ROOM

TRADITIONAL WOODWORKING

THE

CHILDREN'S

ROOM

Step-by-step projects for the woodworker

Watson-Guptill Publications/New York

First published in the United States by

Watson-Guptill Publications

a division of BPI Communications, Inc.

1515 Broadway, New York, N. Y. 10036

Originally published by Collins & Brown Ltd

London House, Great Eastern Wharf

Parkgate Road, London SW11 4NQ

ISBN 0-8230-5404-7

Library of Congress Catalog Card Number: 98-86428

A NOTE ON SAFETY

While the publishers can take no responsibility for the safety of any child using
or playing with the projects presented here, we do advise the following safety precautions:
• Make sure that all nails, woodscrews or other fittings are secure to avoid
the danger of a child swallowing such items or being otherwise injured by them.
• Take extra care when finishing to avoid rough edges.
• Always use child-safe paints (see p. 72).
• Always protect children from wood dust and any potentially
dangerous tools or materials you use when working.

Please also note that, for the purposes of visual clarity in step-by-step photographs,
safety guards on power tools have at times been removed. Always refer to the
manufacturer's safety instructions when working with any power or machine tool.

Series Editor: Liz Dean

Project Editor: Ian Kearey

Editorial Assistant: Lisa Balkwill

Designer: Alison Verity

Original Design: Suzanne Metcalfe-Megginson

Illustrator: Keith Field

Editorial Director: Sarah Hoggett

Art Director: Roger Bristow

Printed in China

First printing, 1998

1 2 3 4 5 6 7 8 9 / 06 05 04 03 02 01 00 99 98

CONTENTS

INTRODUCTION

THE PROJECTS IN this book have been designed by both professional and amateur woodworkers and furniture makers. The craftspeople have been selected for their classic and timeless designs, high-quality craftsmanship, innovative techniques and, not least, the ability to explain precisely how their pieces can be made by others. These inspiring projects are designed to suit a range of woodworking skills, from inexperienced to advanced, and with their clear and detailed instructions, color step-by-step photographs and exploded diagrams, they are well within the grasp of all enthusiastic woodworkers.

Making furniture and other items that will be used by children presents more of a challenge than that made for use in, say, a living room. The pieces are more likely to take a few hard knocks in everyday use, and so the materials must be specifically chosen for strength and durability, rather than for color or attractiveness. This, however, need not be a disadvantage, since it allows you to consider alternative coverings, either to disguise plain surfaces, to match bright existing furnishings, or to make the piece into a colorful focus. The Toy Chest (p. 56) and the Playhouse (p. 24) are large enough to become centerpieces in this way, while some of the other projects, such as the Animal Safari (p. 10) and Character Mobile (p. 68) require more intricate paintwork.

Tools and Materials

The majority of these projects do not require a lot of finely detailed work, yet a good basic set of hand tools, well sharpened and maintained, is essential. Power tools, such as a drill, jigsaw, router and sander, are useful for the more intensive jobs involved. In addition, a small powered fretsaw or jigsaw will prove invaluable when cutting out the shapes for the Teddy Bear Book Ends (p. 36), Caterpillar Peg Rail (p. 64), Animal Safari (p. 10) and Character Mobile (p. 68). However, most of the projects here can be made using hand tools only.

A basic hand-tool kit should consist of a workbench, C and bar clamps, a selection of saws such as the tenon, coping, dovetail and ripsaw, and marking devices such as try squares, steel rules, a mortise gauge, marking knife and pencil. A hammer, mallet, and drill are essential, as are planes, chisels, screwdrivers, and some means of sharpening them. Don't forget a selection of sandpapers, graded from fine to coarse.

The projects in this book are made from solid softwood or hardwood — either commonly available domestic or imported timber — or plywood. Alternative materials are suggested, so that you can make a choice of what to use, based on your preferences, the style of the piece, and how much you wish to spend. It is best to purchase wood from a local lumber yard, rather than a home-improvement store: the choice of woods will be greater, and the yard will often cut the timber to meet the specifications — particularly useful when starting on a large project such as the Playhouse.

On a project like the Rocking Horse (p. 16), consider what wood you will use before purchasing – a little extra money spent on wood with an attractive color or pattern could certainly make the project into a real eye-catcher.

Finishing and Decoration

In all the projects, you have the choice of following the instructions and advice given for that piece, or you can devise your own color scheme or method of finishing. Whatever you choose, it is wise to be aware of safety factors when choosing paints, and so there is a section at the back of the book on purchasing child-safe and non-toxic paints (pp. 72–73).

LEFT: *These colorful teddy bear book ends (p. 36) are easy to construct and can be made with plywood offcuts.*

RIGHT: *The basic design for the Toy Truck (p. 30) can be adapted for both younger and older children.*

Freehand painting, découpage and stenciling are also popular techniques for decorating children's furniture, so a section on stenciling and a stencil alphabet have been included (pp. 74–75) to give you a start; and there's no reason why you can't use any of the finishing techniques presented here on other projects.

Above all, we hope that you will enjoy making the projects in this book, from large to small, and that the children for whom they are made will get many years of pleasure from owning and using them.

ANIMAL SAFARI

*These toy wild animals, easily constructed
from various thicknesses of birch plywood,
are as popular with today's children as they have
been for hundreds of years. You could make
two of each to start a Noah's Ark collection.*

Most animals are made from three pieces only.

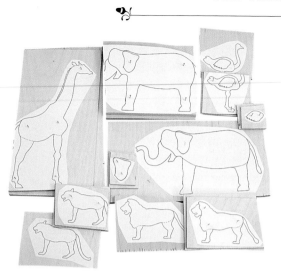

1 Transfer the middle section of each animal onto the relevant thickness of plywood, either by tracing or, as here, by sticking photocopies onto the wood. You can photocopy the animals to different sizes if you prefer. Use a low-tack adhesive for this – a glue stick works well – so that the edges do not lift during fretsawing and the paper can be sanded away easily. Repeat the process for the outer side profiles of each animal and the elephant's ears and the ostrich's wings. Nail each thin piece of plywood onto another of the same thickness, so that you can cut both sides out together, to ensure an identical profile.

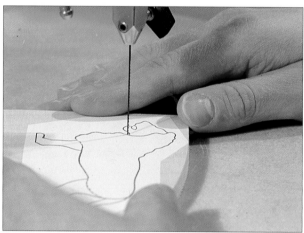

2 Cut out the shapes using a fretsaw; if you use a hand-held one, make sure that the blade does not become angled during cutting. Again, hand-fretsawing thicknesses over $\frac{1}{2}$ in (12 mm) is not advised, so cut out the outer side sections of the elephant and rhinoceros individually. Sand off the glued paper from the middle sections.

Rhinoceros middle

3 Remove the nails from all the nailed sections, sand off the paper, and glue each middle and side section together in the correct order – do not stick the elephant's ears or the ostrich's wings at this stage. PVA, or white woodworking glue, works well, because it allows you to manipulate the sections into place. Clamp each animal in a vice for a few minutes, then remove from the vice and leave to set overnight.

12

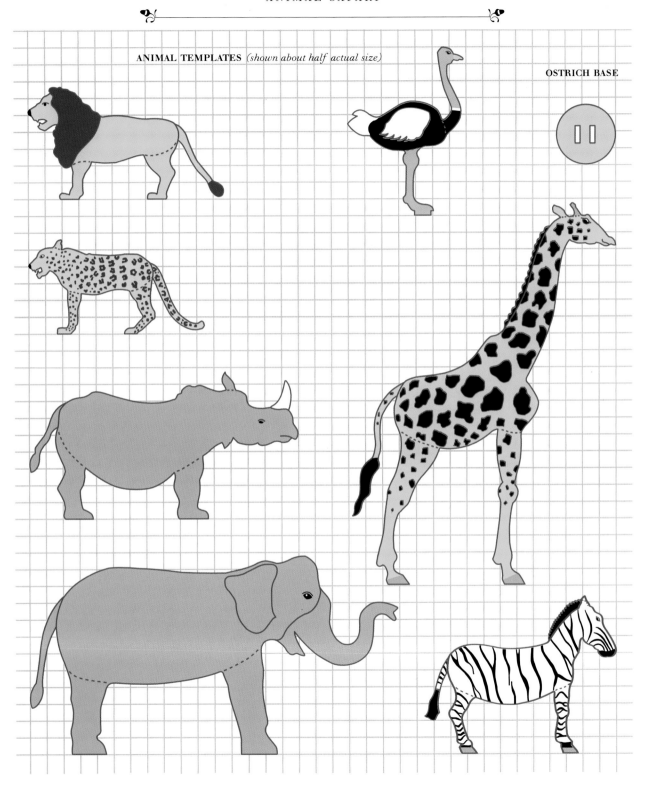

ANIMAL TEMPLATES *(shown about half actual size)*

OSTRICH BASE

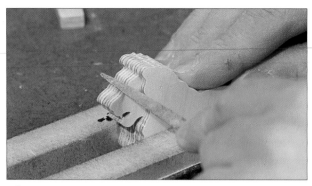

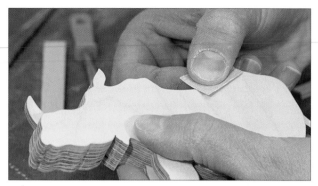

4 When the glue has set, fill the nail holes with filler and clean up any uneven edges with sanding sticks and small files, making any necessary adjustments to the profiles.

5 Glue the elephant's ears and the ostrich's wings in place, clamp and allow to dry as before. You can now round and generally shape the edges of each animal to suit your requirements – for realism, the lion's mane can be left quite rough.

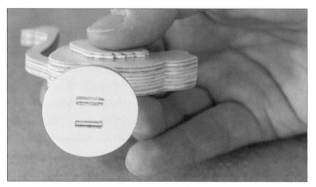

6 For the ostrich's base, mark a 1³⁄₈-in (35-mm) diameter circle onto ¹⁄₈ in (4 mm) scrap plywood and cut it out with a fretsaw. Position the ostrich centrally on the base and mark around the tenon base of each foot. Fretsaw out the 'mortises' and glue the ostrich to the base.

7 Prime and paint the animals – you can either paint them with lifelike colors and details, or use a basic, bright and simplistic color scheme. Enamel gloss paints are the best choice, being hardwearing and quite easily mixed.

Choosing Colors

The following colors were applied to the animals shown here, and represent a basic selection that can be used straight onto the animals, or mixed together to create a range of more subtle shades.

Light buff was used for the base color of the lion and giraffe; tan was applied for the lion's mane and tail hair; mid-brown for the giraffe's patches and hair; bright red for the inside of the lion's and leopard's mouths; black for the eyes, the zebra's stripes, the leopard's spots, the ostrich's feathers, and general detailing. White is the base color of the zebra, the ostrich's feathers and general detailing; pale gray for the base color of the elephant and the rhinoceros, and the zebra's and giraffe's hooves; and yellow for the ostrich's beak and the base color of the leopard. The ostrich's neck and legs were colored using a mixture of white, red and yellow.

LIST OF MATERIALS *(measurements indicate cut size)*		
ITEM	SECTION	LENGTH
GIRAFFE		
Plywood for middle, 1	$5\frac{3}{4}$ x $\frac{1}{2}$ in (145 x 12 mm)	$9\frac{1}{8}$ in (233 mm)
Plywood for sides, 2	$6\frac{1}{4}$ x $\frac{1}{4}$ in (160 x 6 mm)	1 ft 2 in (356 mm)
LION		
Plywood for middle, 1	2 x $\frac{3}{8}$ in (50 x 10 mm)	$4\frac{3}{4}$ in (120 mm)
Plywood for sides, 2	$2\frac{3}{4}$ x $\frac{1}{8}$ in (70 x 4 mm)	$6\frac{1}{4}$ in (160 mm)
LEOPARD		
Plywood for middle, 1	$2\frac{1}{4}$ x $\frac{1}{4}$ in (55 x 6 mm)	$4\frac{1}{4}$ in (110 mm)
Plywood for sides, 2	$2\frac{3}{8}$ x $\frac{1}{8}$ in (60 x 4 mm)	$6\frac{1}{4}$ in (160 mm)
ZEBRA		
Plywood for middle, 1	3 x $\frac{1}{2}$ in (75 x 12 mm)	$4\frac{3}{4}$ in (120 mm)
Plywood for sides, 2	4 x $\frac{1}{8}$ in (100 x 4 mm)	$8\frac{1}{4}$ in (210 mm)
RHINOCEROS		
Plywood for middle, 1	$2\frac{3}{4}$ x $\frac{1}{4}$ in (70 x 6 mm)	$6\frac{1}{2}$ in (165 mm)
Plywood for sides, 2	$3\frac{5}{8}$ x $\frac{3}{8}$ in (93 x 10 mm)	1 ft (305 mm)
ELEPHANT		
Plywood for middle, 1	$3\frac{3}{4}$ x $\frac{1}{4}$ in (95 x 6 mm)	$8\frac{3}{4}$ in (220 mm)
Plywood for sides, 2	$4\frac{3}{4}$ x $\frac{1}{2}$ in (120 x 12 mm)	1 ft $\frac{1}{2}$ in (320 mm)
Plywood for ears, 2	$1\frac{1}{4}$ x $\frac{1}{8}$ in (32 x 4 mm)	$3\frac{1}{2}$ in (90 mm)
OSTRICH		
Plywood for middle, 1	$2\frac{1}{2}$ x $\frac{1}{4}$ in (65 x 6 mm)	3 in (75 mm)
Plywood for sides, 2	$2\frac{3}{8}$ x $\frac{1}{8}$ in (60 x 4 mm)	$5\frac{1}{2}$ in (140 mm)
Plywood for wings, 2	$\frac{7}{8}$ x $\frac{1}{8}$ in (21 x 4 mm)	$2\frac{1}{2}$ in (65 mm)
Plywood for base, 1	$1\frac{3}{8}$ in (35 mm) diameter	$\frac{1}{8}$ in (4 mm)

ROCKING HORSE

*This simple rocking horse, made from
well-seasoned pine, involves no carving
or complicated joints and is glued and screwed
together. The solid traditional safety stand
provides a proper swinging action,
to satisfy the most active riders.*

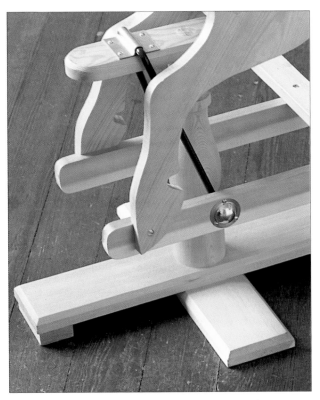

The swing-irons are held on by brass brackets.

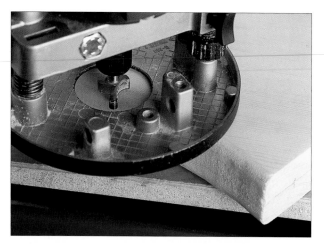

1 The head can be prepared from two pieces, each 5¾ in (146 mm) wide. Glue and clamp together the pieces to make up the head, and when dry, cut to 1 ft 2 in (356 mm) length. Mark out the profile of the head and neck, and cut out – a bandsaw makes this job easier. Round over the edges of the head and neck, using a router with a roundover cutter: do not round over the base that fits along the seat, the front edges of the ears, the inside of the mouth and the nostrils. You can use a spokeshave, a chisel, or a lot of sanding to round over. Mark and drill a ¾ in (19 mm) hole through the neck for the handle. Cut the handle to 8 in (200 mm) length and glue in place. Mark and drill shallow holes for the eyes.

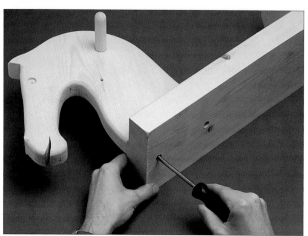

2 Mark and cut the seat to 1 ft 9 in (535 mm) length, and round over the edges, except where the head and rump join it. Mark and cut the rump and seat back to 5 in (125 mm) each, and drill a ¾ in (19 mm) hole in the back of the rump for the tail. Mark and drill pilot holes through the seat for the head and seat back, and through the seat back for the rump. Bevel the bottom of the seat back to fit against the rump. Glue and screw the head and seat back to the seat, and the rump to the seat back, each time recessing the screw heads.

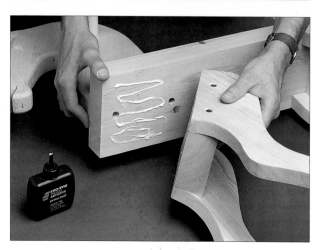

3 Cut the legs to 1 ft 6 in (460 mm), and shape the profiles with a bandsaw, then cut the leg blocks to 5 in (125 mm). Mark and shape a 10° bevel on the top of the legs and the sides of the leg blocks. Glue and screw the legs to the leg blocks, checking the angle, then drill pilot holes through the leg blocks and glue and screw them to the underside of the seat.

4 Mark and cut the plywood body sides to 10½ in (267 mm), and glue and screw them to the insides of the legs, making sure that they fit snugly to the underside of the seat. Cut the hoof rails to 2 ft 10 in (865 mm), and round over the ends; you can also cut bevel edges on the central parts. With the hoof rails standing on their bottom edges, support the legs on pieces of ¼ in (6 mm) scrap wood, and mark and cut out the hoof notches in the hooves; mark the legs and hoof rails to ensure a good fit during assembly, then drill screw holes through the hooves.

5 Whether you turn the posts yourself or buy them ready-turned, mark and cut them to 1 ft 1 in (330 mm) length. Cut the top rail to 2 ft 10 in (865 mm), the bottom rail to 3 ft 5½ in (1054 mm), the cross-pieces to 1 ft 4 in (406 mm) and the bottom rail blocks to 3 in (75 mm). Glue and screw the cross-pieces to the underside of the bottom rail, and then drill a central 1 in (25 mm) dowel hole through both pieces. Glue and screw the bottom rail blocks to the ends of the underside of the bottom rail.

6 Drill 1 in (25 mm) dowel holes through the top rail, and matching holes 2 in (50 mm) deep into the tops and bottoms of the posts. Cut two dowels 4 in (100 mm) long, glue them into the bottom of the posts and glue and wedge them through the bottom rail and cross-pieces. Cut two dowels 3 in (75 mm) long, glue them into the top of the posts, and glue and wedge them through the top rail.

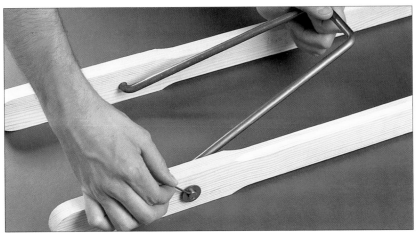

7 Mark and drill holes 6 in (150 mm) from each end of the hoof rails, pass the swing-irons through and fit washers over the ends.

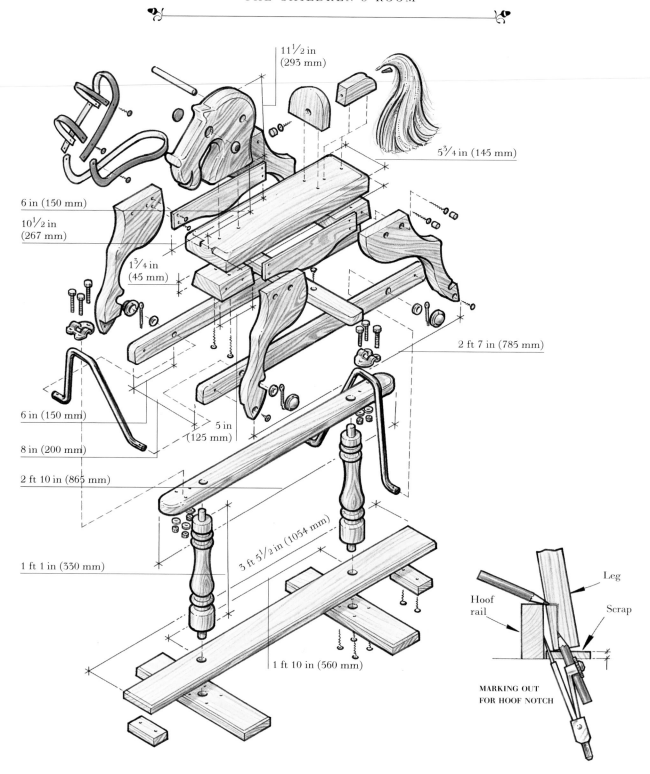

11½ in (293 mm)

5¾ in (145 mm)

6 in (150 mm)

10½ in (267 mm)

1¾ in (45 mm)

2 ft 7 in (785 mm)

6 in (150 mm)

8 in (200 mm)

2 ft 10 in (865 mm)

5 in (125 mm)

1 ft 1 in (330 mm)

3 ft 5½ in (1054 mm)

1 ft 10 in (560 mm)

Leg

Hoof rail

Scrap

MARKING OUT FOR HOOF NOTCH

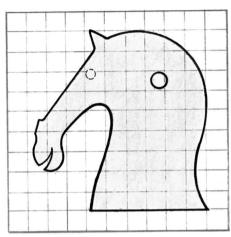

TEMPLATES FOR HEAD,
LEGS AND BODY SIDES

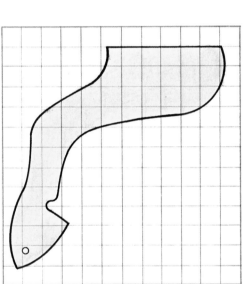

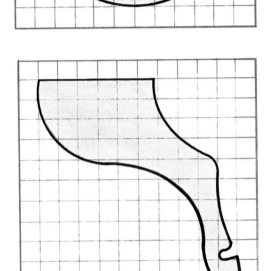

Finishing and Decorating

Apply two or three coats of clear varnish, with a light rub-down between each coat. Fix glass eyes into the socket holes with pine-colored wood filler. (However, if the horse will be played with by children under 3 years do not use glass eyes or any other substitute as small objects are a choking hazard.) Glue simulated horsehair into the hole in the rump, and tap a small wedge underneath the tail for extra strength. To make the bridle and reins, cut strips of $3/8$ in (10 mm) red leather strapping to length and fix them to the head with $1/2$ in (12 mm) brass roundhead screws.

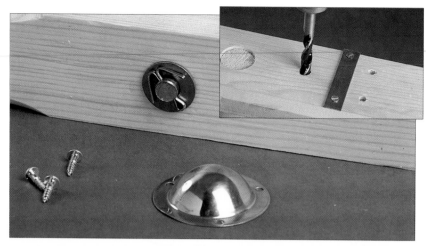

8 Secure the swing-irons with split nails, check that the movement of the swing-irons is easy, then cover the split nails and washers with brass 'derby hat' covers. Screw a steel strip to the top of the top rail, 3 in (75 mm) from each end, for the swing-irons to rest on. Drill screw and bolt holes for the swing-iron brackets. Smear a dab of grease onto the steel strips (see inset).

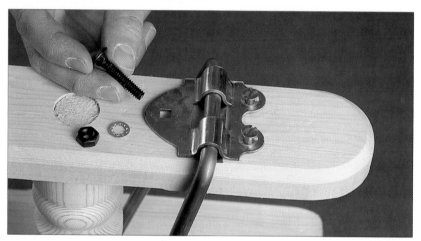

9 Place the tops of the swing-irons on the steel strips. Screw and bolt – using a gripping washer to secure the nut – the top brackets over them, ensuring that the swing-irons swing freely.

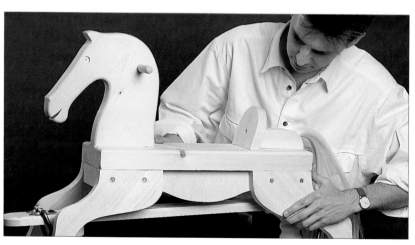

10 Lift the horse onto the hoof rails, and screw the hooves to the hoof rails. Cut the foot rest to 1 ft 6 in (460 mm), round the corners, and screw it crossways onto the hoof rails.

ITEM	SECTION	LENGTH
LIST OF MATERIALS *(measurements indicate cut size)*		
HORSE		
Softwood for head, 1	$11\frac{1}{2}$ x $1\frac{3}{8}$ in (293 x 35 mm)	1 ft 2 in (356 mm)
Softwood for seat, 1	$5\frac{3}{4}$ x $1\frac{3}{4}$ in (145 x 45 mm)	1 ft 9 in (535 mm)
Softwood for handle, 1	$\frac{3}{4}$ in (19 mm) diameter	8 in (200 mm)
Softwood for rump, 1	$1\frac{3}{4}$ x $1\frac{3}{8}$ in (45 x 35 mm)	5 in (125 mm)
Softwood for seat back, 1	4 x 1 in (100 x 25 mm)	5 in (125 mm)
Softwood for legs, 4	6 x $\frac{7}{8}$ in (150 x 21 mm)	6 ft (1840 mm)
Softwood for leg blocks, 2	$4\frac{1}{2}$ x $1\frac{3}{8}$ in (115 x 35 mm)	10 in (255 mm)
Plywood for body sides, 2	4 x $\frac{3}{8}$ in (100 x 10 mm)	1 ft 9 in (535 mm)
Softwood for hoof rails, 2, and foot rest, 1	$1\frac{3}{4}$ x $\frac{3}{4}$ in (45 x 19 mm)	7 ft 2 in (2190 mm)
STAND		
Softwood for posts, 2	3 in (75 mm) diameter	2 ft 2 in (660 mm)
Softwood for top rail, 1, bottom rail, 1, bottom rail blocks, 2, and cross-pieces, 2	4 x 1 in (100 x 25 mm)	8 ft $9\frac{1}{2}$ in (2679 mm)
Hardwood dowels, 4	1 in (25 mm) diameter	1 ft 2 in (356 mm)
Eyes, 2, bridle and reins, 1, and tail, 1		
Steel strips, 2, steel swing-irons, 2,		
Brackets, 2, bolts, 2, washers, 2,		
Split nails, 2, and brass covers, 4, woodscrews		

PLAYHOUSE

This attractive playhouse can be adapted to any dimensions to suit your garden or yard.
The size of the house is slightly larger than the base, to allow moisture to drip off it. The building
uses no joints in its construction, but is screwed and nailed together; the balcony is simply glued.

Baseboard

Pencil guidelines

1 Use the baseboard to mark out in full size the lengths of all the frame components, including the four corner posts; if you use only one face of the base, this can be turned over when assembling the playhouse. Start with the front and back frames, and check the angles are correct.

2 Cut the frame components to length; where duplicate pieces are used in each end, cut double the amount. Fit each component into place, checking that you have cut the dimensions correctly according to the layout on the baseboard.

3 Clamp a couple of components to the baseboard, drill pilot holes, apply glue liberally and screw the components together – hand pressure should hold the joints until the screws hold them. Be careful not to overtighten the joints, because most of them go into end grain. Repeat the process for the two side frames, including the window braces.

4 Cut all the clapboard cladding to length, aiming to use complete boards wherever possible. Position the first piece of clapboard to the bottom of the frame, and nail it along the bottom edge and the top onto each piece of vertical framing. Add the other pieces of clapboard, working from the bottom up and allowing a 1 in (25 mm) overlap on each one, and nailing only along the top edge into the verticals. Cut and nail the boards in place on all four sides of the frame. Cross-cut the timber for the door and window linings to length, and nail into place.

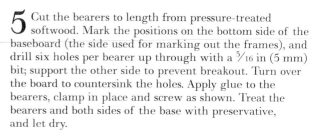

5 Cut the bearers to length from pressure-treated softwood. Mark the positions on the bottom side of the baseboard (the side used for marking out the frames), and drill six holes per bearer up through with a $^3/_{16}$ in (5 mm) bit; support the other side to prevent breakout. Turn over the board to countersink the holes. Apply glue to the bearers, clamp in place and screw as shown. Treat the bearers and both sides of the base with preservative, and let dry.

6 Clamp the corner posts to the ends, allowing them to protrude a little past the cladding, and drill pilot holes and screw into place. You will probably need an assistant to help you with this; once the end frames are joined by one side frame, the assembly can be held with extended bar clamps. Check for square at all stages of assembly.

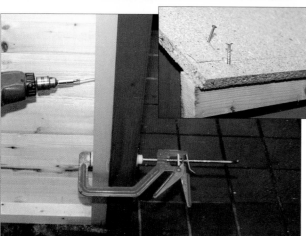

7 Cut the ridge board to length and drop it into place at the top of the end frames. Cut two internal and two external fillets to length. Cut the chipboard for the roof panels slightly oversize, then place the first panel on the pitch of the roof, overhanging the back edge by $^3/_4$ in (19 mm), and nail into place without driving the nails home. Position and nail the second roof panel in place.

8 Hold the internal angled fillets in place and mark a pencil line along the outside. Drill up for fixing screws, countersink the holes from above, apply glue and screw into place. Follow the same procedure for the two outer angled fillets. When in place, trim back the roof panels to finish flush with the outer fillets (see inset).

9 Cut the bearers for the underside of the roof – these fit on the inside and outside of each end, and at the end of the overhanging roof portion. Cut the angles to fit snugly, countersink from above, and glue and screw into place. Use offcuts of roofing felt to pack out the bearers that run up the insides before final fixing.

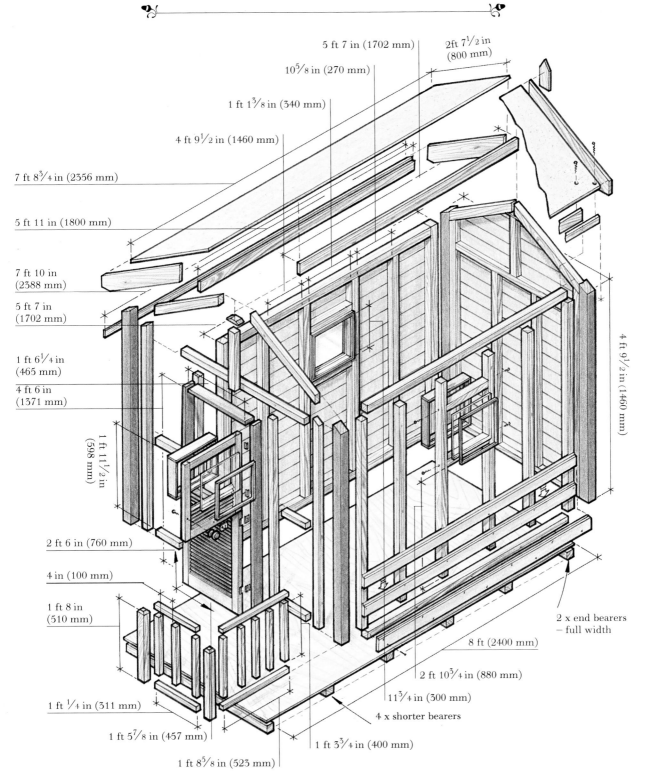

5 ft 7 in (1702 mm)

2ft 7½ in (800 mm)

10⅝ in (270 mm)

1 ft 1⅜ in (340 mm)

4 ft 9½ in (1460 mm)

7 ft 8¾ in (2356 mm)

5 ft 11 in (1800 mm)

7 ft 10 in (2388 mm)

5 ft 7 in (1702 mm)

1 ft 6¼ in (465 mm)

4 ft 6 in (1371 mm)

1 ft 11½ in (598 mm)

4 ft 9½ in (1460 mm)

2 ft 6 in (760 mm)

4 in (100 mm)

1 ft 8 in (510 mm)

2 x end bearers – full width

8 ft (2400 mm)

1 ft ¼ in (311 mm)

2 ft 10¾ in (880 mm)

11¾ in (300 mm)

4 x shorter bearers

1 ft 5⅞ in (457 mm)

1 ft 3¾ in (400 mm)

1 ft 8⅝ in (523 mm)

Clamped
bargeboards

10 Cut the roofing felt oversize, and tack it in place along the sides of the roof. Cut and miter two sets of barge boards and apex molding, if desired, then mark decorations along the bottom edges and cut them out with a jigsaw. Tack the felt under the ends of the roof and screw the barge boards to the roof trusses over the ends of the roof.

11 Cut the corner posts, rails and uprights for the balcony to length. Apply glue to the butt joints, and clamp until the glue sets – make sure that the gaps between the uprights are no more than 4 in (100 mm) apart, so that children's heads cannot get stuck in the gaps.

12 Miter-cut some beading and use it as a rabbet for the clear sheeting in the door and window frames. Trim the sheeting to size, and hold it in place with more miter-cut beading.

13 If you want to put a window in the top ready-made louvre door, cut through the louvres and discard the wood. Cut the tongue off the remaining louvre, and line out the hole with glued and nailed timber. Use miter-cut beading as for the other windows to hold the clear sheeting in position. Fit the doors to the frame with flush hinges, and a door knob and roller catch on each door.

LIST OF MATERIALS *(measurements indicate cut size)*

ITEM	SECTION	LENGTH
Plywood for base, 1	4 ft x $\frac{1}{2}$ in (1220 x 12 mm)	8 ft (2440 mm)
Pressure-treated softwood for base bearers, 6	2 x $1\frac{7}{8}$ in (50 x 47 mm)	32 ft (9760 mm)
Softwood clapboards for cladding, 60	6 x 1 in (150 x 25 mm)	205 ft $5\frac{1}{2}$ in (62.62 m)
Top louvre door, 1, and bottom louvre door, 1	1 ft 6 in x $1\frac{3}{4}$ in (460 x 45 mm)	4 ft 6 in (1371 mm)
Softwood for door knobs, 2		$1\frac{7}{8}$ in (47 mm) diameter
FRAME		
Softwood for verticals, 22, and horizontals (including window braces), 17	$1\frac{3}{4}$ x $1\frac{3}{4}$ in (45 x 45 mm)	136 ft 9 in (41.31 m)
Softwood for door and window linings, 11	$2\frac{3}{4}$ x $\frac{3}{4}$ in (70 x 19 mm)	17 ft $11\frac{3}{4}$ in (5487 mm)
Softwood for corner posts, 4	$2\frac{3}{4}$ x $2\frac{3}{4}$ in (70 x 70 mm)	20 ft (6120 mm)
ROOF		
Chipboard for roof panels, 2	2 ft $7\frac{1}{2}$ in x $\frac{1}{2}$ in (800 x 12 mm)	15 ft $5\frac{1}{2}$ in (4712 mm)
Softwood for roof ridge, 1, and underside bearers, 2	$2\frac{3}{4}$ x $\frac{3}{4}$ in (70 x 19 mm)	19 ft $1\frac{3}{4}$ in (5820 mm)
Softwood for underside bearers, 10, and fillets, 4	$1\frac{3}{4}$ x $\frac{3}{4}$ in (45 x 19 mm)	50 ft (15.24 m)
Softwood for barge boards/fascias, 2	5 x $\frac{3}{4}$ in (125 x 19 mm)	5 ft 8 in (1730 mm)
BALCONY		
Softwood for end posts, 4	$1\frac{3}{4}$ x $1\frac{3}{4}$ in (45 x 45 mm)	6 ft 8 in (2040 mm)
Softwood for rails, 8, and uprights, 16	$1\frac{3}{8}$ x $1\frac{3}{8}$ in (35 x 35 mm)	31 ft $11\frac{1}{2}$ in (9736 mm)
Asphalt roofing felt, galvanized felt nails		
Clear sheeting and beading for windows		
Galvanized cabin hook		
Flush hinges, 4, roller door catches, 2		
Woodscrews, nails, chipboard screws		
Oval bright wire nails		

TOY TRUCK

This sturdy six-wheeler truck features a shape-sorter box and four shapes for younger children. For children under 3 years, the dimensions of the shapes must be increased for safety purposes. The box can be removed for older children, or a piece of plywood can be fitted onto the sorter-box top, and the top glued onto the flatbed.

The cab front is nailed to the chassis.

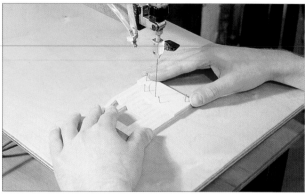

11⁵⁄₈ in (295 mm)

³⁄₁₆ in (5 mm)
diameter axle holes

1 Mark and cut the chassis top and sides to 11⁵⁄₈ in (295 mm) length. Tape or nail the sides together, mark and drill the three ³⁄₁₆-in (5-mm) diameter axle holes through both, and mark and cut them to shape with a fretsaw. Glue and nail the sides to the top; check that the axle holes are in alignment by fitting lengths of axle rod through the holes and placing a wheel onto each end. Rest the chassis on a flat surface and check that all the wheels are in contact with the surface.

2 Cut the cab front to 4³⁄₄ in (120 mm) length, and glue and nail it to the front of the chassis. Mark the cab sides to 4¹⁄₂ in (115 mm) length and cut them to shape with a fretsaw; don't remove the wheel arch shapes yet. Mark the wheel arches to 3¹⁄₂ in (90 mm) and cut them to shape with a fretsaw. Glue the wheel arches to the cab sides, holding them in place temporarily with nails. When the arches are set, cut out the arch shapes on the sides with a fretsaw.

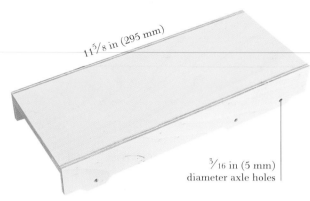

3 Nail and glue the cab sides to the chassis and cab front. Cut the cab back and cab roof to 4³⁄₄ in (120 mm), and nail and glue them into position. To finish the cab, use a block plane to shape the front edge of the roof to make a smooth join. Mark and cut the front bumper to 5¹⁄₂ in (140 mm) and the lights/radiator section to 5¹⁄₄ in (133 mm). On the lights/radiator, drill four ¹⁄₂-in (12-mm) diameter holes for the lights, and cut out four ³⁄₃₂ in (2 mm) slots 2 in (50 mm) long for the radiator grille. Glue and nail the front bumper to the front of the chassis, then position the lights/radiator ³⁄₁₆ in (5 mm) above it and glue and nail into position.

4 Cut the tailgate to 5¹⁄₂ in (140 mm) length, and shape with a fretsaw. Using a fretsaw, cut the 3⁷⁄₈ x ⁵⁄₈ in (98 x 16 mm) hole ⁵⁄₁₆ in (8 mm) above the bottom edge of the tailgate. Cut the flatbed to 8⁷⁄₈ in (225 mm), position it on the chassis sides so that it overlaps them equally, and glue and nail in place. Position the tailgate to meet the bottom of the flatbed, and glue and nail in place. Smooth round the edges with sandpaper, a rasp or file.

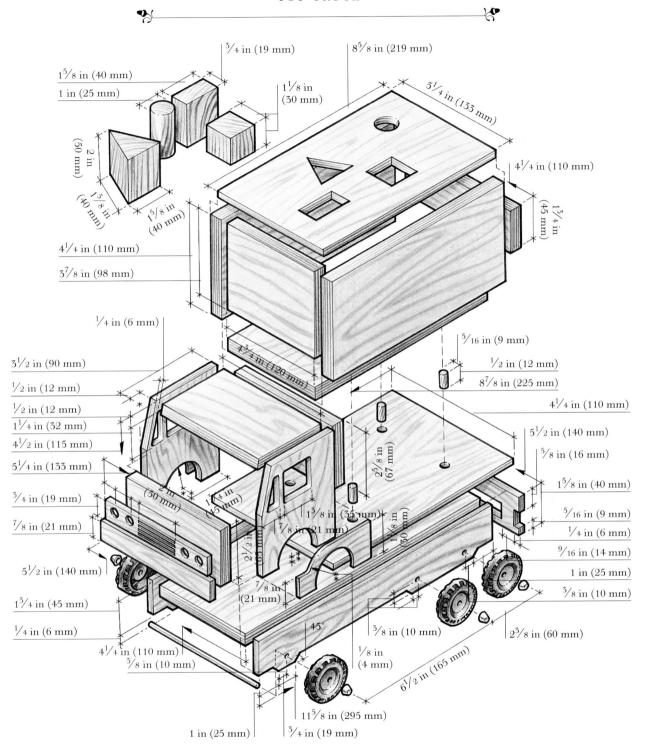

3/4 in (19 mm)

8 5/8 in (219 mm)

1 5/8 in (40 mm)

1 in (25 mm)

1 1/8 in (30 mm)

5 1/4 in (133 mm)

2 in (50 mm)

4 1/4 in (110 mm)

1 3/4 in (45 mm)

1 5/8 in (40 mm)

1 5/8 in (40 mm)

4 1/4 in (110 mm)

3 7/8 in (98 mm)

1/4 in (6 mm)

4 3/4 in (120 mm)

5/16 in (9 mm)

3 1/2 in (90 mm)

1/2 in (12 mm)

1/2 in (12 mm)

8 7/8 in (225 mm)

4 1/4 in (110 mm)

1/2 in (12 mm)

1 1/4 in (32 mm)

2 5/8 in (67 mm)

5 1/2 in (140 mm)

5/8 in (16 mm)

4 1/2 in (115 mm)

5 1/4 in (133 mm)

1 5/8 in (40 mm)

3/4 in (19 mm)

2 in (50 mm)

1 3/4 in (45 mm)

1 3/8 in (35 mm)

1 1/8 in (30 mm)

5/16 in (9 mm)

7/8 in (21 mm)

7/8 in (21 mm)

1/4 in (6 mm)

9/16 in (14 mm)

5 1/2 in (140 mm)

2 1/2 in (65 mm)

7/8 in (21 mm)

1 in (25 mm)

1 3/4 in (45 mm)

3/8 in (10 mm)

1/4 in (6 mm)

45°

3/8 in (10 mm)

1/8 in (4 mm)

2 3/8 in (60 mm)

4 1/4 in (110 mm)

3/8 in (10 mm)

6 1/2 in (165 mm)

11 5/8 in (295 mm)

1 in (25 mm)

3/4 in (19 mm)

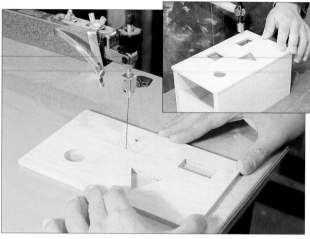

5 Mark out the cube, square, rectangle and triangle to the sizes given in the list of materials (see opposite). Cut out each of the shapes and then smooth and round the edges. You can use a different colored hardwood for each shape, as here, or make all four from the same wood and paint them later.

6 Mark and cut the shape sorter box front and back to $4\frac{1}{4}$ in (110 mm) and the sides and base to $8\frac{5}{8}$ in (219 mm). Plane all the meeting edges square and assemble with glue and nails. Mark and cut the shape sorter box top to $8\frac{5}{8}$ in (219 mm). Mark the profiles of the shapes a fraction larger than the shapes themselves, so that they fit through easily. Cut out the shapes with a fretsaw, clean up the edges, then glue and nail the top to the box (see inset) and round all the edges with sandpaper.

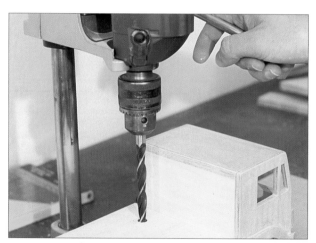

7 Drill four $\frac{5}{16}$-in (9-mm) diameter dowel holes to a depth of $\frac{1}{4}$ in (6 mm) in the base of the box. Fit with dowel markers and use to mark matching holes in the top of the flatbed, then drill dowel holes to $\frac{1}{4}$ in (6 mm) depth. Cut four dowels to $\frac{1}{2}$ in (12 mm) length, and glue into the holes in the box base.

8 Cut three axles to length and tap a spring hubcap on one end of each axle as shown. Put a wheel and then a washer onto the axles, and pass axles through one set of axle holes. Fit a washer and wheel to the other end of each axle, then tap on a spring hubcap to secure.

LIST OF MATERIALS *(measurements indicate cut size)*		
ITEM	SECTION	LENGTH
TRUCK		
Birch plywood for chassis top, 1	$4\frac{1}{4}$ x $\frac{1}{2}$ in (110 x 12 mm)	$11\frac{5}{8}$ in (295 mm)
Birch plywood for chassis sides, 2	$1\frac{3}{4}$ x $\frac{1}{4}$ in (45 x 6 mm)	1 ft $11\frac{1}{4}$ in (590 mm)
Birch plywood for cab front, 1	$2\frac{1}{2}$ x $\frac{1}{2}$ in (65 x 12 mm)	$4\frac{3}{4}$ in (120 mm)
Birch plywood for cab sides, 2	$3\frac{1}{2}$ x $\frac{1}{4}$ in (90 x 6 mm)	9 in (230 mm)
Birch plywood for cab back, 1	$2\frac{5}{8}$ x $\frac{1}{2}$ in (67 x 12 mm)	$4\frac{3}{4}$ in (120 mm)
Birch plywood for cab roof, 1	$3\frac{1}{8}$ x $\frac{3}{8}$ in (80 x 10 mm)	$4\frac{3}{4}$ in (120 mm)
Birch plywood for wheel arches, 2	$1\frac{11}{16}$ x $\frac{1}{8}$ in (42 x 4 mm)	7 in (178 mm)
Birch plywood for front bumper, 1, and lights/radiator, 1	$\frac{7}{8}$ x $\frac{1}{4}$ in (21 x 6 mm)	$10\frac{3}{4}$ in (273 mm)
Birch plywood for tailgate, 1	$1\frac{5}{8}$ x $\frac{1}{4}$ in (40 x 6 mm)	$5\frac{1}{2}$ in (140 mm)
Birch plywood for flatbed, 1	6 x $\frac{1}{4}$ in (150 x 6 mm)	$8\frac{7}{8}$ in (225 mm)
SHAPE SORTER BOX		
Birch plywood for base, 1, and sides, 2	$4\frac{1}{4}$ x $\frac{1}{2}$ in (110 x 12 mm)	2 ft $1\frac{7}{8}$ in (657 mm)
Birch plywood for back, 1	$1\frac{3}{4}$ x $\frac{1}{2}$ in (45 x 12 mm)	$4\frac{1}{4}$ in (110 mm)
Birch plywood for front, 1	$3\frac{7}{8}$ x $\frac{1}{2}$ in (98 x 12 mm)	$4\frac{1}{4}$ in (110 mm)
Birch plywood for top, 1	$5\frac{1}{4}$ x $\frac{1}{4}$ in (133 x 6 mm)	$8\frac{5}{8}$ in (219 mm)
SHAPES AND WHEELS		
Ramin dowel for cylinder, 1	1 in (25 mm) diameter	2 in (50 mm)
Mahogany for triangle, 1	$1\frac{5}{8}$ x $1\frac{5}{8}$ in (40 x 40 mm)	2 in (50 mm)
Beech for cube, 1	$1\frac{1}{8}$ x $1\frac{1}{8}$ in (30 x 30 mm)	$1\frac{1}{8}$ in (30 mm)
Oak for rectangle, 1	$1\frac{5}{8}$ x $\frac{3}{4}$ in (40 x 19 mm)	2 in (50 mm)
Hardwood dowels, 4	$\frac{5}{16}$ in (9 mm) diameter	
Axles, 3, and plastic wheels, 6	$\frac{3}{16}$ in (5 mm) diameter	
Spring hubcaps, 6	2 in (50 mm) diameter	
Molding pins	$\frac{3}{4}$ and 1 in (19 mm and 25 mm)	

TEDDY BEAR BOOK ENDS

These teddy bear book ends provide a decorative way of keeping books neatly on a surface or shelf. They are easy to construct, using dowel joints and screwed butt joints, and can be made with softwood and plywood offcuts.

The profiles are cut out with a fretsaw.

1 You can either photocopy the two teddy bear shapes and enlarge them to the correct dimensions, or draw them freehand. Here, each bear is drawn separately on paper to 6¼ in (160 mm). Cut out the shapes and glue them onto ⅛ in (4 mm) birch plywood as shown.

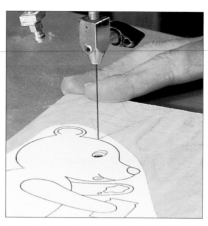

2 Carefully cut around the character shapes using a powered fretsaw or hand fretsaw. With sandpaper wrapped around a sanding block, sand off the paper and smooth the surfaces. Next, clean up all the edges by working around them with sandpaper or a small file.

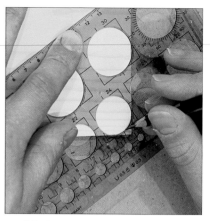

3 Mark and cut the two softwood bases to 5½ in (140 mm), and the two uprights to 8 in (200 mm). Leave the corners square, or mark corner curves and cut out using a fretsaw or jigsaw. In each base, mark the two screw holes for the bears, then drill and countersink the pilot holes.

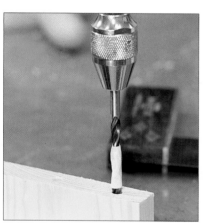

4 Cut six 1 in (25 mm) lengths from ¼-in (6-mm) diameter fluted hardwood doweling. Mark the position for the three dowel holes on the meeting edge of each base. Attach a piece of sticky tape ½ in (12 mm) from the tip of a ¼ in (6 mm) drill bit, and drill the dowel holes to the depth shown by the sticky tape.

5 Insert brass dowel markers into the dowel holes, then position the base meeting edge to the face of the matching upright and press the two pieces together. Using the same marked drill bit, drill the dowel holes in the uprights. Glue and insert the dowels, then clamp the uprights and bases together and let dry.

6 Place each bear on its base, then push an awl or bradawl through the pilot screw holes to mark the hole positions on the bears' bottom edges. Drill pilot holes in the bears and screw each to its base. Undo screws, remove the bears and paint them using child-safe paints (see p. 72). Apply a finish to the bases and uprights. When dry, screw the bears to the bases.

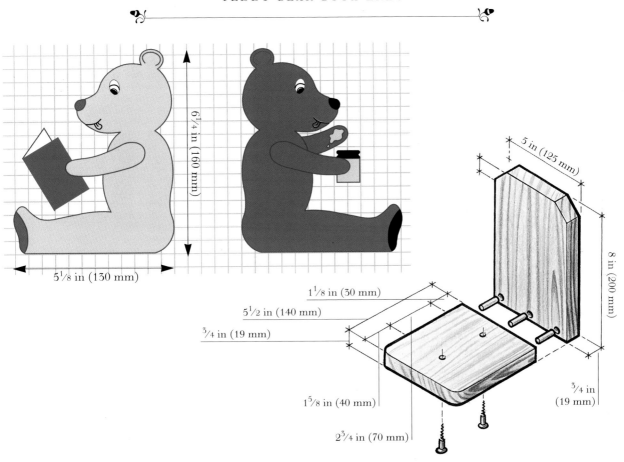

$6^{1}/_{4}$ in (160 mm)

$5^{1}/_{8}$ in (130 mm)

$1^{1}/_{8}$ in (30 mm)

$5^{1}/_{2}$ in (140 mm)

$^{3}/_{4}$ in (19 mm)

$1^{5}/_{8}$ in (40 mm)

$2^{3}/_{4}$ in (70 mm)

5 in (125 mm)

8 in (200 mm)

$^{3}/_{4}$ in (19 mm)

LIST OF MATERIALS *(measurements indicate cut size)*		
ITEM	SECTION	LENGTH
Birch plywood for teddy bears, 2	$5^{1}/_{8}$ x $^{1}/_{8}$ in (130 x 4 mm)	1 ft $^{1}/_{2}$ in (320 mm)
Softwood for uprights, 2, and bases, 2	5 x $^{3}/_{4}$ in (125 x 19 mm)	2 ft 3 in (680 mm)
Fluted hardwood dowels, 6	$^{1}/_{4}$ in (6 mm) diameter	6 in (150 mm)
No. 6 countersunk screws, 4	$1^{1}/_{4}$ in (32 mm)	
Baize, felt, or sheet cork		
Brass dowel markers		

PINE BED

The basic frame of this versatile bed is sturdily constructed from softwood, using mortise-and-tenon joints and bed bolts, knock-down fittings that are easily assembled. You can vary the design of the headboard and finials to add a personal touch.

You can turn the finials or buy them ready-made.

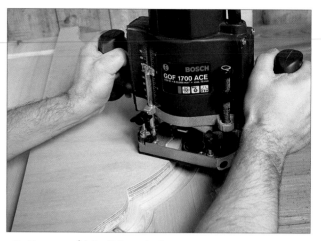

1 Mark and cut the boards for the headboard to slightly over 3 ft 3 in (990 mm), and for the footboard to slightly over 3 ft 2⅛ in (968 mm). Plane the meeting edges square and cut for joining, using either a biscuit joiner and beech biscuits, dowels, or loose-tongue joints. Apply glue and clamp with bar clamps.

2 Cut out a ½ in (12 mm) plywood template for the head-board top edge, then mark this on the headboard. Cut the top edge to shape. Use the same template to guide a router and decorative cutter for the molding profile on the headboard's top edge. Add laminate to the template to bring it to 1 in (25 mm), then use a router guide to cut the same decorative groove on the face of the headboard, curved at the top and straight along the sides and bottom.

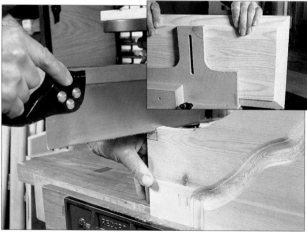

3 Next, sand the entire headboard piece using an orbital sander, and finish by carefully sanding along the grain by hand. Make sure that you smooth away any torn grain along the router cuts.

4 Cut a ½-in (12-mm) square notch at the top of the headboard sides to fit into the corner-post mortises. Using a router, field the footboard edges to ½ in (12 mm), to fit into mortises in corner posts and end rails (see inset).

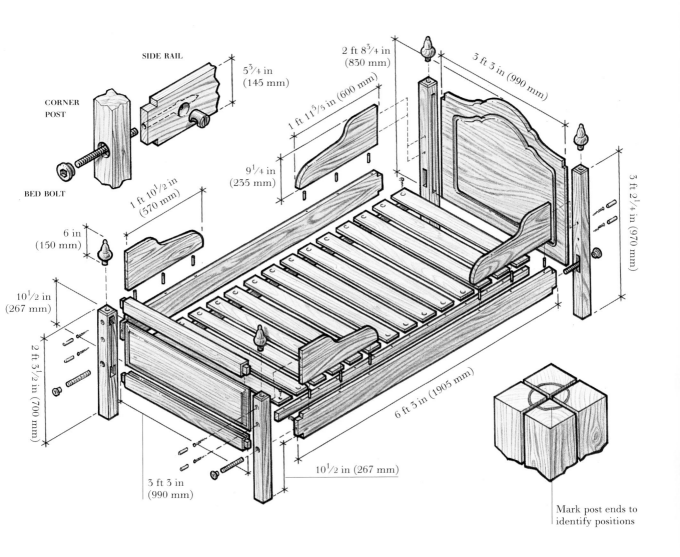

SIDE RAIL

5³/4 in
(145 mm)

CORNER
POST

BED BOLT

2 ft 8³/4 in
(830 mm)

3 ft 3 in (990 mm)

1 ft 11⁵/₈ in (600 mm)

9¹/4 in
(235 mm)

3 ft 2¹/4 in (970 mm)

1 ft 10¹/2 in
(570 mm)

6 in
(150 mm)

10¹/2 in
(267 mm)

2 ft 3¹/2 in (700 mm)

6 ft 3 in (1905 mm)

3 ft 3 in
(990 mm)

10¹/2 in (267 mm)

Mark post ends to
identify positions

Finishing

If you want to add variety when using pine or another pale softwood, water-based stains are available in a wide range of colors. Make sure that you stain and finish the reduced edges of the footboard before fixing it dry into position within the grooves of the end rails and corner posts. This way, if the footboard shrinks, it will not expose a white line of unfinished wood. Finish with varnish or seal the wood before waxing it.

5 Cut the head corner posts to 3 ft 2¼ in (970 mm) and the foot corner posts to 2 ft 3½ in (700 mm), and plane or sand the surfaces smooth. Make pencil marks on the posts to avoid confusion when marking out for jointing. Mark 4 x 1 in (100 x 25 mm) mortises starting 10½ in (267 mm) from the bottom of each corner post for the side rails, and chop out, using a mortise or bevel-edged chisel, or drill out waste wood and clean up with a chisel. Again starting 10½ in (267 mm) from the bottom of each corner post, cut out the ¾ in (19 mm) mortise for the headboard and the ½ in (12 mm) mortises for the footboard as shown.

6 Cut the end rails to 3 ft 3 in (990 mm), and cut 1½ in (38 mm) tenons flat on each end. Cut ½ in (12 mm) grooves for the footboard along the bottom edge of the top end rail and the top edge of the bottom end rail. At each end of the footboard mortises on the foot corner posts, chop out 1½ in (38 mm) mortises for the end rail tenons. Cut the side rails to 6 ft 3 in (1905 mm) and cut 4 in (100 mm) tenons on each end. Dry-assemble the entire frame, checking for square and making any adjustments, then mark matching components and disassemble.

7 Drill the holes for the bed bolts through the corner posts, using an electric drill and stand. Dry-assemble the corner posts and side rails, mark through the holes onto the side rail tenons and then hand-drill the bed bolt holes into the side rails. Carefully bore the recess for the nut in the inside face of the side rails, then make a trial fitting of the bed bolts and nuts, tightening until the shoulders of the rail tenons pull up square against the corner posts. Undo the bolts and disassemble.

8 Drill a ⅝ in (16 mm) dowel hole into the bottom of each finial as shown. Mark the center of the top of each corner post, and drill a matching dowel hole. Chamfer all the top and side edges of the corner posts, then glue in the dowels to the finials and post tops. Round over all sharp corners, using a router fitted with an ovolo cutter. Glue the headboard into the mortises in the head corner posts and clamp with bar clamps. Dry-fit the footboard into the grooves in the end rails, then glue up the end-rail tenons into the foot corner post mortises, and hold with bar clamps. Clean off surplus glue and let dry. Next, cut the slat rails to 6 ft 1⅞ in (1868 mm) and place along the side rails so the slats will be below the top edge; the height will be determined by the thickness of your mattress. Drill pilot holes and screw slat rails into place.

9 Assemble the frame and tighten the bed bolts. Cut the slats to 3 ft $^3/_8$ in (925 mm), and space evenly along the slat rails. Staple the slats to two lengths of webbing, then screw the head- and foot-end slats into place. Cut the head side panels to 1 ft 11 $^5/_8$ in (600 mm) and the foot side panels to 1 ft 10$^1/_2$ in (570 mm). Make a template for their shape, and cut with a jigsaw or bandsaw. Drill three dowel holes in the bottom edge and matching holes in the top edge of the side rails, and two pilot holes for each panel through the corner posts. Glue in the dowels and glue and screw the panels to the side rails and corner posts. Make rounded pegs and fit into the countersunk screw holes, to hide the screw heads.

LIST OF MATERIALS *(measurements indicate cut size)*

ITEM	SECTION	LENGTH
Softwood for head corner posts, 2, and foot corner posts, 2	2$^1/_2$ x 2$^1/_2$ in (65 x 65 mm)	10 ft 11$^1/_2$ in (3340 mm)
Softwood for side rails, 2	5$^3/_4$ x 1 in (145 x 25 mm)	12 ft 6 in (3825 mm)
Softwood for slat rails, 2	1$^3/_4$ x 1 in (45 x 25 mm)	12 ft 3$^3/_4$ in (3750 mm)
Softwood for head side panels, 2, and foot side panels, 2	9$^1/_4$ x $^3/_4$ in (235 x 19 mm)	7 ft 8$^1/_4$ in (2340 mm)
Softwood for end rails, 2	3 x 1$^3/_4$ in (75 x 45 mm)	6 ft 6 in (1987 mm)
Softwood for headboard, 1	2 ft 8$^3/_4$ in x $^3/_4$ in (830 x 19 mm)	3 ft 3 in (990 mm)
Softwood for footboard, 1	10$^1/_2$ x $^3/_4$ in (267 x 19 mm)	3 ft 2$^1/_8$ in (968 mm)
Softwood for slats, 14	3$^1/_2$ x $^5/_8$ in (90 x 16 mm)	42 ft 5$^1/_4$ in (12.95 m)
Softwood for finials, 4	2 x 2 in (50 x 50 mm)	2 ft (600 mm)
Dowels, 12 and 4 respectively	$^3/_8$ in (10 mm), $^5/_8$ in (16 mm) diameter	
Bed bolts, 4, wooden pegs, 12		
Beech biscuits, woodscrews, webbing		

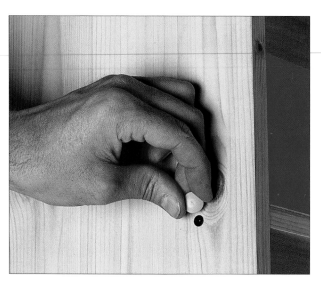

4 Press screw cappings onto the screw heads, to disguise them. Wood-finish melamine looks best with matching cappings, but with colored, black or white melamine, contrasting cappings can also look good.

5 Cut the melamine-faced hardboard for the back to size, then nail it to the back of the unit, spacing the nails at approximately 8 in (200 mm) intervals; again, you can use matching or contrasting colors.

LIST OF MATERIALS (measurements indicate cut size)		
ITEM	SECTION	LENGTH
Melamine-faced chipboard for sides, 2	1 ft 2 in x $^9/_{16}$ in (356 x 14 mm)	12 ft (3680 mm)
Melamine-faced chipboard for shelves, 6	1 ft 1$^3/_4$ in x $^9/_{16}$ in (350 x 14 mm)	15 ft 2$^1/_4$ in (4620 mm)
Melamine-faced chipboard for top, 1	1 ft 2 in x $^9/_{16}$ in (356 x 14 mm)	2 ft 6$^3/_8$ in (770 mm)
Melamine-faced chipboard for kickboard, 1	3 x $^9/_{16}$ in (75 x 14 mm)	2 ft 6$^3/_8$ in (770 mm)
Melamine-faced hardboard for back, 1	2 ft 7 in x $^1/_4$ in (785 x 6 mm)	6 ft (1840 mm)
Chipboard screws and cappings, 30	2 in (50 mm)	
Panel nails	1 in (25 mm)	
Edging tape		

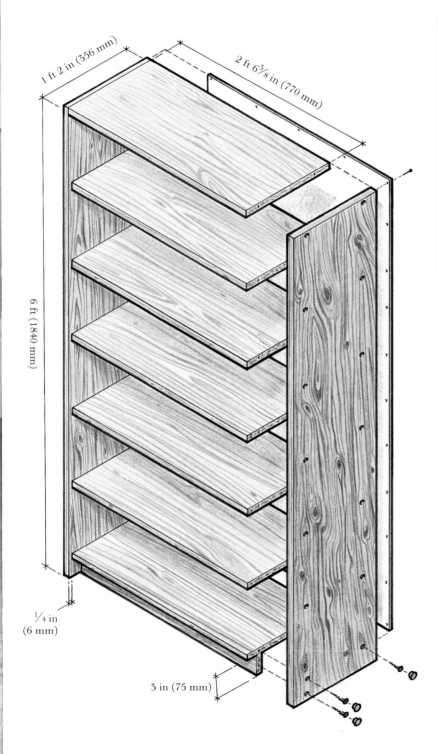

1 ft 2 in (356 mm)

2 ft 6³⁄₈ in (770 mm)

6 ft (1840 mm)

¹⁄₄ in (6 mm)

3 in (75 mm)

Using Chipboard

Some of the advantages of using chipboard are that it is light, inexpensive and, when faced with any of a large range of melamine or hardboard veneers, easy to clean; in addition, it does not need to be finished or maintained. It is widely available in different widths and thicknesses, and is a standard material for many kitchen and bedroom fittings. However, it does not take ordinary woodscrews well, so you have to use special chipboard ones, and once damaged, a piece cannot be repaired.

1 Mark out the components onto the plywood: the table front and back legs are 1 ft 7⅝ in (500 mm), the table side legs 1 ft 6½ in (470 mm), the chair front legs 11¾ in (300 mm) and the chair side legs 10⅜ in (265 mm). Draw the various radii with a template to 2 in (50 mm), except for the back of the chair seat, which is ⅞ in (21 mm) and the seat back hole, which is 2⅜ in (60 mm).

2 Cut all the components to length. Make all the major straight cuts with a circular saw, using a guide bearer to ensure accuracy. Make the internal cuts for the leg components with a jigsaw, and sand their internal edges.

3 Use a ⅜ in (10 mm) round-over bit on both sides of the internal edges. These can simply be rounded-over, or the bit can be set to form a rabbet detail, as shown here.

4 Round over both top and bottom edges of the table top and chair seat. Don't rout any edge which will form an external corner – this is much easier to do after assembly.

5 Start the seat back hole with a spade bit, and cut out the rest of the hole with a jigsaw. Sand and then finish both sides of the hole using the router fitted with the round-over bit.

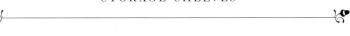

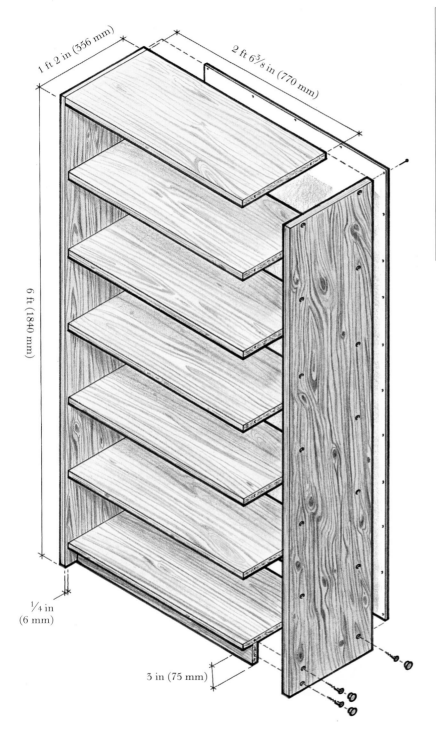

1 ft 2 in (356 mm)

2 ft 6⅜ in (770 mm)

6 ft (1840 mm)

¼ in
(6 mm)

3 in (75 mm)

Using Chipboard

Some of the advantages of using chipboard are that it is light, inexpensive and, when faced with any of a large range of melamine or hardboard veneers, easy to clean; in addition, it does not need to be finished or maintained. It is widely available in different widths and thicknesses, and is a standard material for many kitchen and bedroom fittings. However, it does not take ordinary woodscrews well, so you have to use special chipboard ones, and once damaged, a piece cannot be repaired.

CHILD-SIZE TABLE SET

This solid table-and-chair set is constructed using biscuit joints, and its design includes rounded features for added safety for children. With careful planning, a table and one chair can be made from a single sheet of plywood. You will need to use more for extra chairs.

The seat hole is rounded using a router.

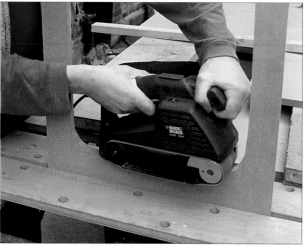

1 Mark out the components onto the plywood: the table front and back legs are 1 ft 7⅝ in (500 mm), the table side legs 1 ft 6½ in (470 mm), the chair front legs 11¾ in (300 mm) and the chair side legs 10⅜ in (265 mm). Draw the various radii with a template to 2 in (50 mm), except for the back of the chair seat, which is ⅞ in (21 mm) and the seat back hole, which is 2⅜ in (60 mm).

2 Cut all the components to length. Make all the major straight cuts with a circular saw, using a guide bearer to ensure accuracy. Make the internal cuts for the leg components with a jigsaw, and sand their internal edges.

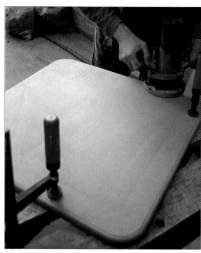

3 Use a ⅜ in (10 mm) round-over bit on both sides of the internal edges. These can simply be rounded-over, or the bit can be set to form a rabbet detail, as shown here.

4 Round over both top and bottom edges of the table top and chair seat. Don't rout any edge which will form an external corner — this is much easier to do after assembly.

5 Start the seat back hole with a spade bit, and cut out the rest of the hole with a jigsaw. Sand and then finish both sides of the hole using the router fitted with the round-over bit.

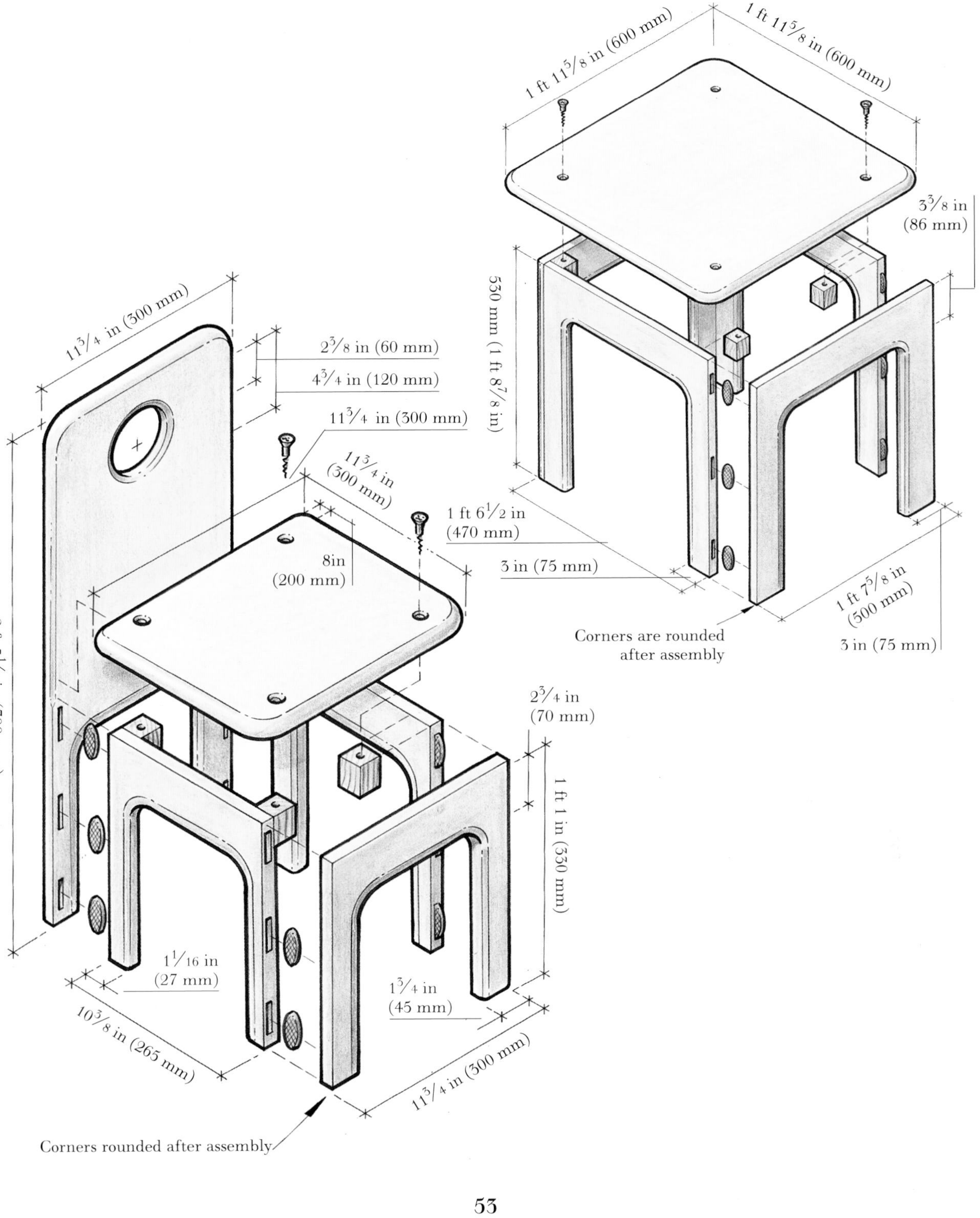
1 ft 11⅝ in (600 mm)
1 ft 11⅝ in (600 mm)
3⅜ in (86 mm)
530 mm (1 ft 8⅞ in)
1 ft 6½ in (470 mm)
3 in (75 mm)
1 ft 7⅝ in (500 mm)
3 in (75 mm)
Corners are rounded after assembly
11¾ in (300 mm)
2⅜ in (60 mm)
4¾ in (120 mm)
11¾ in (300 mm)
11¾ in (300 mm)
8in (200 mm)
2 ft 3½ in (700 mm)
2¾ in (70 mm)
1 ft 1 in (330 mm)
1 1/16 in (27 mm)
1¾ in (45 mm)
10⅜ in (265 mm)
11¾ in (300 mm)
Corners rounded after assembly

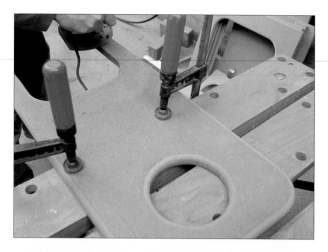

6 Rout the internal edges of the chair back legs, and rout the front external edge. This edge should only be routed to within ⅝ in (16 mm) of the top of the chair seat. Once again, leave the back edge to be routed after assembly. Plane smooth any rough edges, to ensure that all external corners will be true.

7 The legs are assembled with beech biscuits and glue. Cut the biscuit slots in the meeting edges of the components, allowing for three No. 10 biscuits on each joint. Apply glue and insert the biscuits.

8 When clamping up the leg assemblies with bar clamps, it is a good idea to ask a friend to help. Here, the table top is held onto the assembly so that its position can be marked.

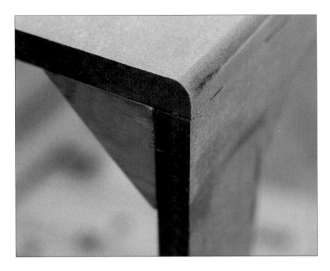

9 When the leg assemblies are dry, cut small blocks of pine offcuts to 2¾ in (70 mm) and glue them into place. You can either leave them square or shape them to fit into the internal corners, as illustrated here. Round over all the external corners of the leg assemblies, then use woodscrews to attach the table top and chair seat to the wooden blocks. Cover the screw heads with filler and sand smooth.

LIST OF MATERIALS *(measurements indicate cut size)*		
ITEM	SECTION	LENGTH
TABLE		
Plywood for top, 1	1 ft 11⅝ in x ¾ in (600 x 19 mm)	1 ft 11⅝ in (600 mm)
Plywood for front and back legs, 2, and side legs, 2	1 ft 8⅞ in x ¾ in (530 x 19 mm)	6 ft 4¼ in (1940 mm)
CHAIR		
Plywood for seat, 1	1 ft 1⅜ in x ¾ in (340 x 19 mm)	11¾ in (300 mm)
Plywood for front legs, 1, and side legs, 2	1 ft 1 in x ¾ in (330 x 19 mm)	2 ft 8½ in (830 mm)
Plywood for back, 1	2 ft 3½ in x ¾ in (700 x 19 mm)	11¾ in (300 mm)
Pine for corner blocks, 8	2¾ x ⅝ in (70 x 16 mm)	1 ft 10 in (560 mm)
No. 8 woodscrews	1½ in (38 mm)	
No. 10 beech biscuits		

TOY CHEST

*This useful and easily constructed toy storage chest uses only butt joints, glued
and nailed together, with some decorative molding to provide visual interest.
The carcass and lift-off lid use plywood, a stable and inexpensive material.*

1 Using a T-square for accuracy, mark the carcass front
and back to 2 ft 6 in (760 mm) length, the sides to
1 ft 5⅞ in (457 mm), and the base to 2 ft 5 in (737 mm).
Score along the lines with a craft knife, to help the saw
follow the lines accurately.

2 Cut the plywood to the correct dimensions using
a hand saw – this produces less dust flying around
the workshop than a power saw. Clean up the edges,
making sure that they are all square and flat.

3 Working from the base as a guide, glue and assemble
the base, sides, front, and back. Clamp up the carcass,
and check that the right angles are accurate. To secure the
joints further, drill pilot holes for nails along the edges,
and hammer in the nails.

4 The joints for the front, back and sides can be given
additional strength by cutting strips of right-angle
molding to length and gluing them into the four inside
corners. Make sure that the top of each strip
is flush with the top of the carcass.

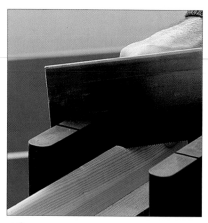

5 Measure and cut the chamfered softwood molding for the corner joints around the base to length, using a miter block or miter saw.

6 Apply glue to the chamfered molding and press it into position around the base, making sure that the mitered joints fit well together. For added strength, drill pilot holes and drive nails through the molding.

7 Mark, score, and cut the lid to 2 ft 6 in (760 mm) length, and clean up the edges. Measure and miter-cut the half-round softwood molding for the lid edges. Apply glue and place the molding in position, holding it with adhesive tape, then drill pilot holes and nail into place. Clean up the whole box to finish.

LIST OF MATERIALS *(measurements indicate cut size)*

ITEM	SECTION	LENGTH
Plywood for front and back, 2, sides, 2, and base, 1	1 ft 5$^7/_8$ in x $^1/_2$ in (457 x 12 mm)	10 ft 4$^3/_4$ in (3171 mm)
Plywood for lid, 1	1 ft 7 x$^1/_2$ in (485 x 12 mm)	2 ft 6 in (760 mm)
Softwood for corner strings	$^1/_2$ in (12 mm) right-angle section	5 ft 9$^1/_2$ in (1764 mm)
Softwood half-molding for lid	$^1/_2$ in (12 mm) diameter	5 ft 8$^1/_4$ in (1730 mm)
Softwood chamfered molding for base	1$^7/_8$ x $^5/_8$ in (47 x 16 mm)	8 ft 6$^1/_8$ in (2595 mm)
Panel nails		

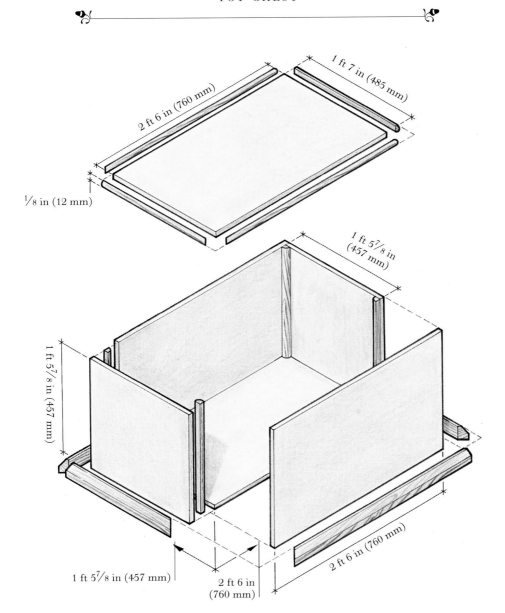

2 ft 6 in (760 mm)

1 ft 7 in (485 mm)

1/8 in (12 mm)

1 ft 5⅞ in (457 mm)

1 ft 5⅞ in (457 mm)

1 ft 5⅞ in (457 mm)

2 ft 6 in (760 mm)

2 ft 6 in (760 mm)

Finishing and Decorating

The relatively characterless surface of plywood makes it a good vehicle for paint finishes after you have filled any gaps and to cover the pinholes, although you can stain it or even consider practicing graining or combing techniques. Using non-toxic paints (see p. 72), you can paint it to match the decor of the child's room or go in for bold, colorful contrasts. Stenciling or hand-lettering are popular alternatives, particularly if you personalize a project with a child's name. Alternatively, you could apply cut-out decorations and then varnish over the whole box.

DRAWING EASEL

*This easel combines a chalk board on one side and a solid panel on the other,
for drawing or painting paper to be clipped to. The frames are constructed using
T-lap joints, and the shelf stops hold the frames in the correct open position.*

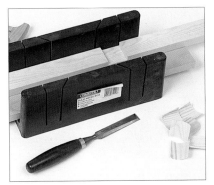

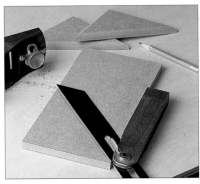

1 Mark and cut the four vertical frame components to 4 ft (1220 mm) and the four horizontals to 1 ft 9 in (535 mm). Mark the lap part of the T-lap joints on the ends of the horizontals, and the matching recesses on the verticals. Cut the joints, using a tenon saw and miter block for accuracy, then clean up the waste in the recess.

2 Glue and clamp the frame components, making sure that the verticals and horizontals are parallel to each other. To facilitate this, cut the boards to 2 ft (610 mm) and clamp them in place temporarily while the glue dries.

3 Set a sliding bevel to 45° and use it to mark the angles for the four corner triangles, then cut them to 4 in (100 mm).

4 Use sandpaper and a sanding block to round over the edges of the triangles and the two boards, starting with a medium-grade and finishing with a fine-grade sandpaper. Check the width between the frame verticals, and cut the shelf to 2 ft (610 mm) length.

5 Miter-cut the half-round beading to fit along the top edges of the shelf, and glue it in place; you can reinforce it with small nails. Glue the triangles in place on the top corners of the frames, and glue the boards in position, again reinforcing with nails.

6 Lay the completed frames on a flat surface with their top edges touching, screw the flap hinges into place, and stand the easel upright. Cut the shelf stops to 1 ft 5 in (430 mm) and use a sliding bevel to calculate the slope to be chamfered on them. Use a plane to cut the chamfer.

7 Glue and clamp the stops parallel and equidistant on the underside of the shelf, ensuring that the chamfer makes the stops slope outwards to keep the easel from opening out too far. Drill pilot holes through the stops into the shelf, and reinforce the joint with screws.

LIST OF MATERIALS *(measurements indicate cut size)*		
ITEM	**SECTION**	**LENGTH**
Softwood for frame verticals, 4, frame horizontals, 4, and shelf stops, 2	2 x 1 in (50 x 25 mm)	25 ft 10 in (7800 mm)
Plywood for boards, 2	1 ft 8 in x $^5/_{16}$ in (510 x 9 mm)	4 ft (1220 mm)
Plywood for shelf, 1	1 ft 5 in x $^5/_{16}$ in (430 x 9 mm)	2 ft (610 mm)
Plywood for triangles, 4	4 x $^5/_{16}$ in (100 x 9 mm)	1 ft 4 in (400 mm)
Half-round softwood beading	1 in (25 mm) wide	6 ft 10 in (2080 mm)
Brass flap hinges, 2	2 in (50 mm)	
Panel nails, woodscrews		

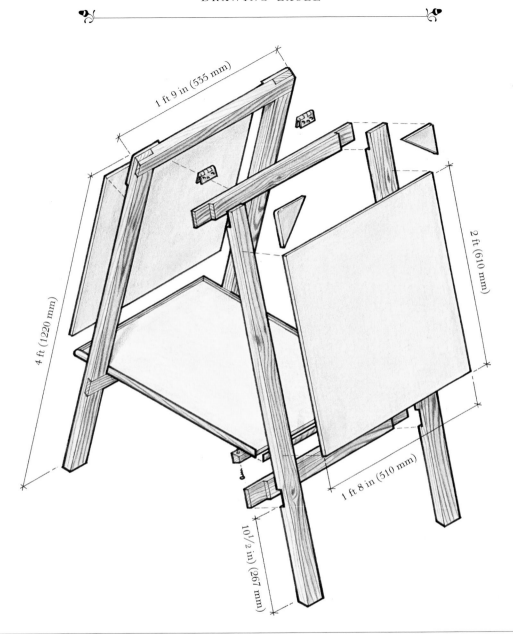

1 ft 9 in (535 mm)

4 ft (1220 mm)

2 ft (610 mm)

1 ft 8 in (510 mm)

10½ in (267 mm)

Finishing

Although you can paint and varnish the whole easel after final construction, it may be easier and more effective to finish the parts as you go along: apply clear or colored varnish to the two frames after you have glued them, and paint the plywood components — *the triangles, boards and shelf — with child-safe paints before you glue them to the frames. You can paint the whole shelf in one color after the beading has been attached, or you can paint the beading a contrasting color.*

CATERPILLAR PEG RAIL

*This friendly caterpillar is an ideal storage
solution for a child's bedroom or playroom
– its three pegs can hold clothes, toys,
shoe bags and more. The body is cut out
with a fretsaw, and the pegs and dowels
can be bought ready-turned.*

The nose screw secures the rail to the wall or door.

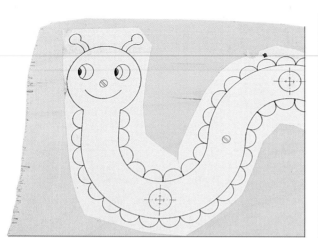

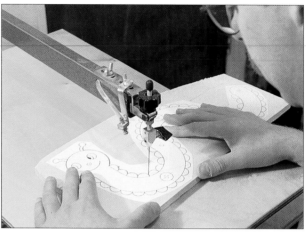

1 Either photocopy the diagram of the caterpillar (see right) and enlarge it to the correct dimensions, or you can draw it freehand onto paper. Cut out your drawing and then glue it onto a piece of ½ in (12 mm) birch plywood.

2 Use a powered or hand fretsaw to cut out the caterpillar profile, taking care to shape the curves consistently. Mark the positions of the fixing screws on the body, and drill clearance holes for No. 6 screws; the screw for the nose is a roundhead one, so countersink only the other three holes.

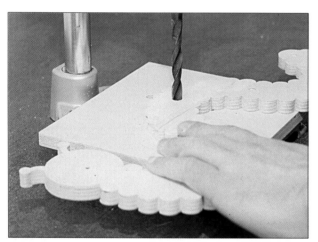

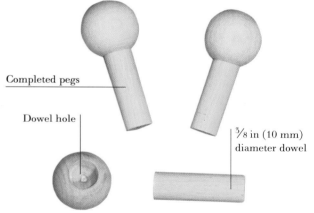

Completed pegs

Dowel hole

⅜ in (10 mm) diameter dowel

3 Mark and drill three ⅜ in (10 mm) holes in the caterpillar body for the pegs as shown. Wrap sandpaper around a sanding block and then sand the guide drawing off the body, making sure that the surface is even. Smooth away any unevenness from the edges of the body, using sandpaper and small files.

4 You can either turn a dowel rod to ⅜ in (10 mm) diameter, or purchase it ready-made. Sand it smooth and cut three 1⅛ in (30 mm) lengths from it. Again, the three ¾-in (19-mm) diameter hardwood balls can be turned or purchased; drill a ⅜ in (10 mm) hole ⅛ in (6 mm) deep in each ball, and glue in a length of dowel. When it is completely dry, glue the pegs into the dowel holes in the body.

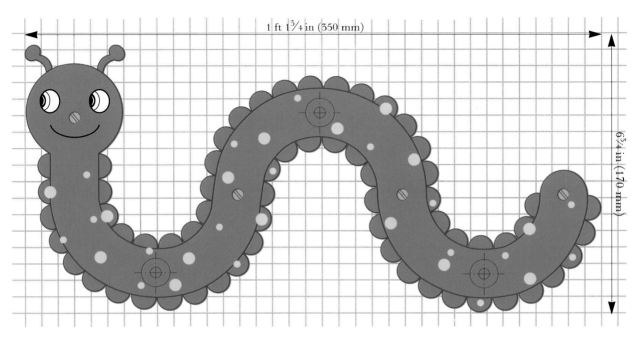

1 ft 1³⁄₄ in (350 mm)

6³⁄₄ in (170 mm)

LIST OF MATERIALS *(measurements indicate cut size)*		
ITEM	**SECTION**	**LENGTH**
Birch plywood for body, 1	6³⁄₄ x ¹⁄₂ in (170 x 12 mm)	1 ft 1³⁄₄ in (350 mm)
Hardwood dowels, 3	³⁄₈ in (10 mm) diameter	3¹⁄₂ in (90 mm)
Hardwood balls, 3	³⁄₄ in (19 mm) diameter	
No. 6 countersunk screws, 3		
No. 6 roundhead screw, 1		

Finishing and Fixing

You can paint or stain the caterpillar in any colors you choose, although green and yellow are probably the most obviously suitable – as always with objects for children's rooms, make sure that the finishing material you use is suitable for toys.

To fix the caterpillar, position it on a wall or door and mark and drill the holes. If you are fixing to a wall, insert wall plugs. Use the three countersunk screws for the body, and the roundhead screw for the nose – this can be painted when it is secure.

CHARACTER MOBILE

*This colorful mobile brightens up
any child's room, with its cloud hangers
and five flying characters cut out
from thin plywood. You can adapt
the theme to your child's favorite
characters, making sure that
you test them for balance first.*

Use a range of child-safe paints in primary colors.

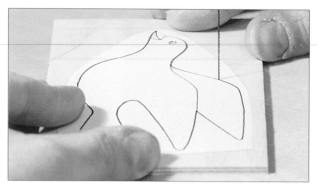

1 Either photocopy the characters and enlarge them to the correct dimensions, or draw them freehand. Here, the bee is 3 x 2⅜ in (75 x 60 mm), the kite 3⅞ x 2⅝ in (98 x 67 mm), the butterfly 4¼ x 2½ in (110 x 65 mm), the bird 5 x 3⅛ in (125 x 80 mm) and the sun 5 x 5 in (125 x 125 mm). Cut out the shapes and glue them onto ⅛ in (4 mm) birch plywood.

2 Cut out the characters using a powered or hand fret-saw, then drill a small hole as shown in each for the hanging thread – the thickness of the hole will depend on the thickness of the thread. Also drill a hole for the tail of the kite. Using sandpaper around a sanding block, sand off the paper and smooth the surfaces, then go around the edges with sandpaper or small files.

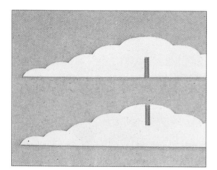

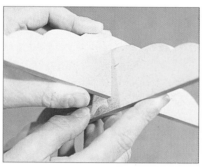

3 Either photocopy the two hangers and enlarge them to 1 ft 1 in (330 mm) length, or draw them freehand. Cut out the shapes and glue them to ¼ in (6 mm) birch plywood, then cut them out with a fretsaw. Sand and smooth the edges. Mark and cut the slots for the halving joint, and pare away any surplus waste wood with a sharp chisel, or file the slots to fit.

4 Drill a small hole at the ends of the hangers as shown, for the thread for the characters. Again, the thickness of the hole will depend on the thickness of the thread. Apply glue to the slots and assemble the hangers, making sure that they are at right angles to each other.

5 When completely dry, paint the hangers and the characters, using child-safe paints (see p. 72). Cut ribbon or shiny paper for the kite tail, and attach it. Screw the curtain eyelet to the top of the assembled hangers, and the small eyelet centrally to the underside.

Hanging the Mobile

First, cut lengths of strong thread for each character. Hang the characters from the hangers, with one hanging from the small central eyelet. Screw either a cup hook or a large eyelet to the ceiling, then cut the cord to length. Tie it to the ceiling eyelet and the curtain eyelet on top of the hangers.

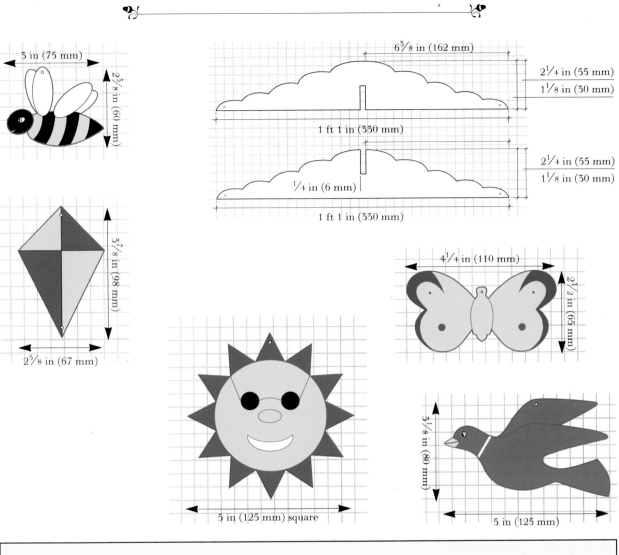

3 in (75 mm)

2³/₈ in (60 mm)

6³/₈ in (162 mm)

2¹/₄ in (55 mm)

1¹/₈ in (30 mm)

1 ft 1 in (330 mm)

2¹/₄ in (55 mm)

1¹/₈ in (30 mm)

¹/₄ in (6 mm)

1 ft 1 in (330 mm)

3⁷/₈ in (98 mm)

2⁵/₈ in (67 mm)

4¹/₄ in (110 mm)

2¹/₂ in (65 mm)

3¹/₈ in (80 mm)

5 in (125 mm) square

5 in (125 mm)

LIST OF MATERIALS *(measurements indicate cut size)*		
ITEM	**SECTION**	**LENGTH**
Birch plywood for characters, 5	5 x ¹/₈ in (125 x 4 mm)	1 ft 3³/₄ in (400 mm)
Birch plywood for hangers, 2	2¹/₄ x ¹/₄ in (55 x 6 mm)	2 ft 2 in (660 mm)
Curtain eyelet, 1, and small brass eyelet, 1		
Thread, cord, and ribbon or shiny paper		

SAFE PAINTS AND STENCILING

The manufacture of "child-safe" paints has been developed in response to public demand for non-toxic coverings for children's toys and furniture. The old art of stenciling is ideal for personalizing an item for your child.

Stenciling
You can stencil with crayon, wax, paint and stains. Work from the outside in for an even effect.

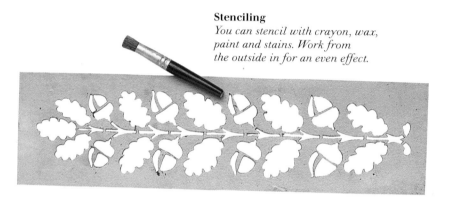

Safe paints
Safe paints are non-toxic and environmentally friendly.

Safe Paints

When choosing paint for children's projects it is important to have a basic understanding of the contents of the paint you use to avoid bringing children into contact with potentially harmful substances.

Paint consists of pigments ground in binders, which form the paint film after the solvents in which the binders are dissolved have evaporated. The binder, also known as polymer, can be made from oils and resins and may be soluble in solvents such as mineral spirit; acrylic emulsion resins are dispersed in water.

Paint manufacturers are very aware of the possible harmful effects of their products, both to the person who applies the paint and to the person who uses the painted object – no paint produced for the USA domestic market now contains added lead, but there could be traces of other metals, and these could cause harm if a child were to suck on or bite a toy or furniture that had been painted. Nearly all manufacturers' catalogs provide some information on the toxicity and safety of the products, and the paints themselves are, for the most part, clearly labeled. Although the majority of regulations were first produced for industry and for professional firms, they are there to help protect anyone who uses the products. For example, when finishing toys or furniture that may come in for some hard and sometimes unorthodox treatment, it is a wise move always to use the safest and most relevant standard child-safe paints.

There is, however, no one single, internationally recognized classification system. As a result, different countries have different standards for child-safe paints and varnishes. In the USA, materials are checked by an independent toxicologist, working in conjunction with the ASTM (American Society for Testing and Materials), and are then graded and labeled by the ACMI (Art and Craft Materials Institute).

In addition, some companies have also begun to respond to growing concern about the effect on the environment of chemical products and by-products. This awareness has given rise to use alternative methods of producing paint. In most cases, this has meant returning to traditional, natural ingredients, and manufacturers of such "organic" paints are quick to point out that their products are safe for use on toys and children's furniture, and can be used by people who are sensitive or allergic to regular paints and finishes. An added advantage is that they do not seal the wood like modern gloss and emulsion paints, but rather allow it to "breathe", thereby eliminating the problem of trapped moisture. However, these alternatives are still noticeably more expensive than regular paints, due to the cost of the natural ingredients and the smaller amounts that are currently produced, and they are not always easy to find. There are companies which specialize in these paints but manufacturers that produce regular paints are beginning to offer "organic" ranges.

Preparing and Working with Paints

Whatever the paint you purchase, and whatever the various uses you intend to put it to, make sure that you follow the manufacturer's instructions − particularly where safety procedures are involved. For example, if you plan to spray paint onto a project, always make sure that you take adequate precautions − such as goggles or face mask, respirator, or disposable gloves. It makes absolutely no sense to spend time making a toy or piece of children's furniture and then to risk damaging your or the child's health, just for the sake of speed or an easy life.

If you need to remove old paint before repainting with paint that conforms to toy safety regulations, this should be removed carefully, because it may contain lead, and the resulting dust or flakes could give rise to the poisoning effects that lead produces. Children up to the age of five are at the greatest risk of contamination from the toxic side effects, one of these being impaired brain development, which can permanently impair mental functions.

To avoid contamination by dust, do not rub down old paint with sandpaper − this will only put lead-rich dust into the air and throughout the house. Either rub the old paint down using wet-and-dry sandpaper with water, or use a chemical paint stripper. Ideally, remove the old paint in an outdoor space to minimize the risk of dust contamination − always wear protective clothing while doing this. If you decide to use a hot-air gun, do this with great care, so as not to cause the paint to burn. Even though it may appear to be the quickest option, do not use a blow torch because this will create fumes when the paint is burnt. The paint that has been removed should be put into a sealed bag and placed in a household trash can; it should not be burned.

It is important to remember that paints that comply with toy safety regulations are only safe when they are dry. While it is still in the liquid form, paint should be kept out of the reach of children; in addition, ensure that there is good ventilation in the room where it is being applied, and that you allow the paint to dry fully before using the toy or piece of furniture.

Stencil brushes
Stencil brushes have short bristles cut to give a flat edge for stippling and dabbing. Use non-toxic products at all times.

Repeating patterns
Make sure that you have worked out the meeting points or corners before stenciling, to avoid overlaps or clashes.

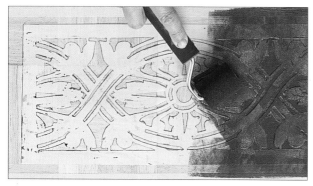

Using a roller
For stenciling large areas or using repeated designs on a floor or wall, a roller can be useful, so long as you remove excess paint.

Checking the stencil
Whatever technique you use, it is vital to partly remove the stencil at one end or corner, to check that the effect is as you want it.

Stencil Brushes and Paints

Stencil brushes are produced specially for the purpose, and using other types of brushes just will not work. The stiff, short bristles are square-cut to give a flat edge that is designed for the stabbing action necessary for stenciling. Most brushes have metal ferrules, but some are intended for water work and are made without the ferrule. As with all brushes, it is advisable to buy the best that you can afford — cheap ones bought for the sake of economy will not last long, and brushes that are well maintained should continue to give good service for a long time. It is also possible to use small rollers for one-color stencils.

Paints used for stenciling need to be fast-drying — special stencil paints are available, but the same results can be obtained from standard water-based acrylic paints. These can be used straight from the can or jar, or you can mix your own colors. The essential point to remember is not to dilute the paint, otherwise it can creep under the stencil and ruin all your good work.

Making Stencils

There is a great variety of commercially produced stencils available, ranging from the simple to the complex; some can be purchased from art and craft stores, while others can be found in books containing copyright-free stencil designs. However, there is no reason why you can't make your own stencils — perhaps to fit a particular piece of furniture — and once you get started, you will find the process of creating designs a fascinating one. Before photocopying printed designs or tracing them from other stenciled furniture, make sure that you are not infringing any copyright laws.

If you use stenciling card, just draw the design straight onto it and cut out the design carefully, using a sharp craft knife or scalpel. Alternatively, draw the design onto a piece of paper and use this as a template for a piece of clear acetate. Lightly tape the acetate over the template, and cut out the design with the knife or scalpel.

Applying the Paint

Before stencilling on a finished piece of woodwork, experiment on scrap wood, cardboard or paper, so that you get a feel for stenciling. The best results are made on wood that has been sealed first, or on already painted surfaces. Tape the stencil in place on the wood – masking tape allows it to be lifted and repositioned easily – or use repositioning glue. If you intend to use the same stencil as a repeating motif, mark out the fixing positions before starting.

Whether you use a stencil brush or roller, the rule is to underload it with paint rather than overload it; you will find that surprisingly little is needed. Wipe or dab the bristles on scrap paper before you begin, to remove any excess paint. Use a stippling action through the stencil, working in from the cut edges; aim to produce an even covering, and be prepared to reload the brush at frequent intervals. As you go along, partly remove the stencil to check you are happy with the effect; replace it carefully and carry on. When you have finished, remove the stencil and allow the paint to dry fully. Because the layer of stenciled paint is quite fragile, it is a good idea to protect it with a layer or two of clear varnish.

Further Techniques

You can vary the depth of color by applying more or less paint in required places, and by using stencils as a base for painting by hand – when the stenciled paint is dry, use fine artist's brushes to add details, shading or contrasts.

Although it is the standard medium, you don't have to use paint when stenciling – two other media are woodstains and colored waxes. Water-based stains create a more transparent effect, where the grain of the wood can be seen under the color. Make sure that the stencil is fixed to prevent any seeping under, and dab the brush on scrap paper after loading, to ensure that you have not overloaded it. Experiment with overlapping colors gently, adding a second color on top of the first, using a clean stencil brush for each color.

A delicate sheen can be achieved by mixing pigments with neutral or clear wax. Use a stencil brush to mix the wax and colored pigment, remove any excess from the bristles, and rub the brush onto the wood from the sides of the stencil, to avoid build-up. This technique looks particularly good with blended colors and simple designs – again, protect the finished stencil with clear varnish or shellac.

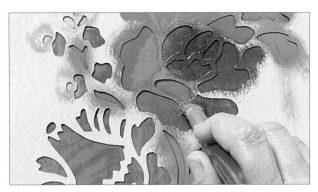

Using colors
Experiment with using different colors on the same stencil, and practice creating deeper or lighter shades for variety.

Using stains
The secret of success with stains is to make sure that you only have a little on the brush, and to use simple designs.

Stenciling with wax
Using pigments allows you to create subtle shades and to make delicate blends and overlaps.

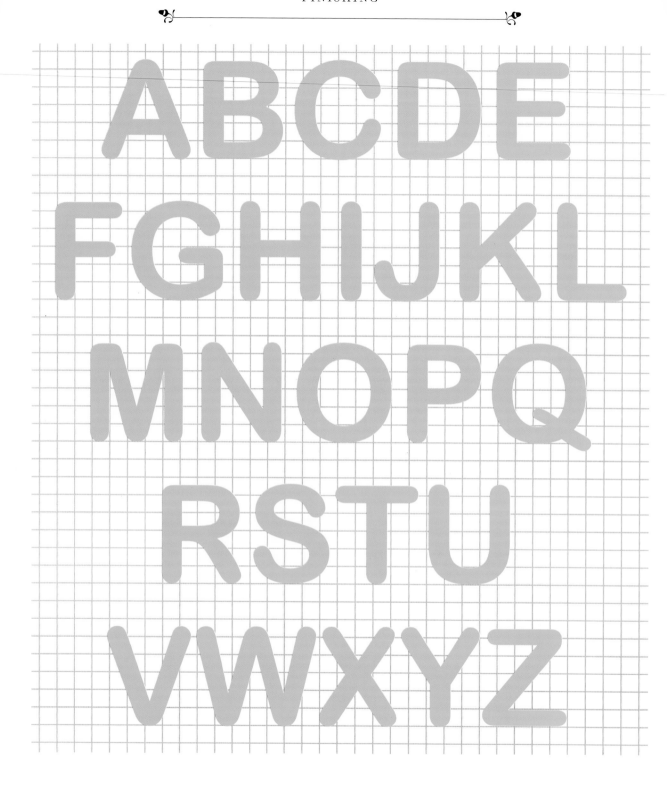

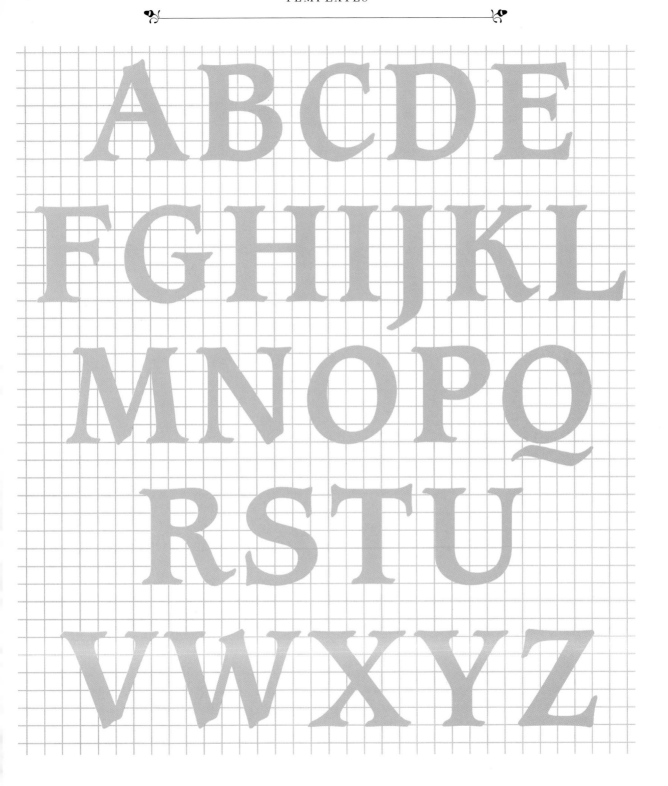

INDEX